SNOOKER

CHARACTERS

JOHN IRELAND'S

SNOOKER
CHARACTERS

TEXT BY
TED LOWE

Macdonald
Queen Anne Press

Queen Anne Press

First published in Great Britain in 1989 by Queen Anne Press,
a division of Macdonald & Co (Publishers) Ltd
1 New Fetter Lane, London EC4A 1AR

A member of Maxwell Pergamon Publishing Corporation plc

British Library Cataloguing in Publication Data

Lowe, Ted
Snooker Characters.
1, Snooker
I. Title II, Ireland, John
794.7'35

ISBN 0-356-17932-X

Made by Lennard Books Ltd

Editor Michael Leitch
Designed by Pocknell & Co
Typeset by Jigsaw Graphics
Printed and bound in Spain by
Grupo Nerecan

CONTENTS

INTRODUCTION

Characters are part of everyday life; the world would be a duller place without them. They appear in every walk of life – some extrovert, some introvert, and over the years billards and snooker have had their fair share. In this book John Ireland has brought a new and marvellously life-like dimension to our 'potty' cueists both past and present.

Potting is a term to describe one ball knocking another into a pocket, but that is not the whole essence of the game, particularly in the three-ball game of billards. Here you have other scoring points such as cannons – one ball contacting the other two; and hazards – a ball entering a pocket after contact; or sending the ball into a pocket as in 'potting'. The origin of billards is very obscure.

One train of thought is that billards was an indoor version of croquet – the mallet replaced by the mace – a wooden stick with a wooden head. The game could have French origins for it is known that Louis XI enjoyed billards on his own table. One thing is certain – billards is a very old game and must have had its characters in the 1400s. After all, Louis XI's table would have had a wooden bed – the slate bed didn't arrive until the 1830s. Can you imagine Messrs Higgins or Knowles playing on a wooden bed for the World Championship!!

It is generally accepted that the first billards professional was John Roberts in the mid 19th century. Other characters of the day were William Cook, William Mitchell and W.J. Peall. They and some other members of the trade set up the Billiards Association in 1885, and so the Official Rules of the game were introduced.

Up to the 1900s other challengers came forward, among them such names as Diggle, Dawson, Stevenson and Aiken, but Roberts stood supreme. A new era was born in the early 1900s through the characters of Inman and Reece. The rivalry between the two became legendary. The stories of their bickering are unlimited. I like the one told following an Inman fluke. Sarcastically Reece asked, 'How did you do that?' Inman snapped in reply, 'You are fully aware of my terms for tuition!' It is considered that Inman was the better player; but it was Reece who played two sessions a day for five weeks to compile a break of 499,135 using the anchor cannon – yes, they changed the rules after that!

In 1920 one of the 'greats' entered the scene – Willie Smith, whose game was that of the ordinary club player but so much better, and quite different to his predecessors. He took over the world title from Melbourne Inman who had held it the previous four years. Smith's confederates were Claude Falkiner, Tom Newman, Freddie Lawrence and Tom Tothill. At this same time three names were to emerge, never to be forgotten, in the history of billiards and snooker: New Zealand's Clark McConachy, Australia's Walter Lindrum and England's Joe Davis.

McConachy, Lindrum and Davis, together with Smith and Newman, literally took over the world stage of billiards until its death in 1934. Davis took the crown from Newman and held it for four years; Smith persuaded the left-handed

Australian to come to Britain following the tragic death of his young wife; Lindrum's magical control of the balls and his break-building speed at close cannons brought monotony for spectators; such was Lindrum's artistry, it is said, anyone could throw three balls on the table, and in three shots Lindrum would get close cannons from the position left by the throw. He was, and always will be, the 'daddy' of the three-ball game.

It was back in 1875 that a young Army officer, Colonel Sir Neville Chamberlain (no relation to the man with the umbrella), while stationed in India had the idea of adding coloured balls to their usual game of Pyramids, so-called because it consisted of a pyramid of red balls, which they took turns to pot with the white cue-ball. The name 'snooker' was an Army term, meaning 'loser' – if you failed to pot the colours you lost your money. Snooker was born.

For many years this variation on pool continued as a fun game, a bit of a joke, something to amuse at the end of a serious billiards match. Not until 1927 did it take on serious overtones. Even then some professionals couldn't accept it – Tom Reece and Willie Smith voiced scathing remarks about the game at regular intervals.

One player however saw the potential in the game of snooker. Joe Davis was not only a champion billiards player, he was an astute businessman and talented organiser. With 22 balls and a variation of colour, he foresaw the busy action of this 'fun-game', and its possibilities. He knew, for he was champion, that the three-ball game of billiards was becoming monotonous to the

spectator, small areas of the table being used for close cannons, and lack of movement causing loss of popularity. He lobbied his fellow pros and friends in the trade to attack the controlling body for a World Snooker Championship. They were reluctant but gave their consent, and fifty-seven years from the inauguration of the billiards championships, professional snooker launched its championship in 1927.

All the history books will tell you how Joe dominated the game for twenty years undefeated – how he built its popularity, how he made the game his own – but those books may not tell you how the game died in 1957 from lack of support and finance. The home of the professional game, Leicester Square Hall (formerly Thurstons) had closed its doors in 1955; the 'shop window' was lost. The three champions of the Fifties and Sixties, Walter Donaldson (twice), Fred Davis (eight times), and particularly John Pulman (eight times over eleven undefeated years) struggled to keep the game alive against all odds, including a new kind of entertainment called television. So difficult was it for Pulman, he set up challenge matches for his title, and survived seven, the number of years there were no championships. Very few of today's players would know about, or even understand, those difficult times.

Oddly enough, the small box called TV, which had played havoc with many entertainments, was to be snooker's salvation. In 1969 'Pot Black' appeared on the screens and was an instant success. It introduced snooker to a new audience, a section of the community hitherto ignorant of the game. Recorded over three and a half days per programme, directed by Jim Dummigham and painstakingly edited by Producer Reg Perrin, 'Pot Black' was shown all over the world. It became its own executioner – each series of sixteen programmes was shown weekly over four months. The overwhelming popularity of its 30-minute air-time attracted a host of sponsors into the game, founding new tournaments that eventually made 'Pot Black' surplus to requirements. New TV tournaments were being interrupted by its four-month run, and consequently the decision was taken to bring it to an end after eighteen years. To its final curtain 'Pot Black' attracted an audience of millions.

Television has, of course, brought the biggest boom the game has ever seen. It has made mega-stars of some players and household names of many more, including the referees. Tournament prize-money now runs into millions of pounds annually, and the playing calendar is so full, contestants sometimes find difficulty in getting from one venue to the next. The life of today's snooker star is very different from that of his predecessor, with managers to deal with everyday mail, organise hotels, and arrange travel, whether it be in the UK or to Hong Kong, and minders/chauffeurs to ensure protection and safety at all times – a far cry from the daily chores of the pre-war professional.

Thankfully, times have changed for the better for all of us. Sometimes to reflect on the past can make one a more appreciative person. Especially now, when to focus on and plan for the future also brings a certain satisfaction. To look at some specific aspects, arrangements are already in hand for ranking tournaments (events open to all members of the WPBSA) to be staged worldwide, in Australia, Bangkok, Dubai, Europe and Canada. Plans are afoot for other parts of the globe. A contract signed by the BBC guarantees the excitement and drama of big tournaments in Great Britain until 1996, and the Crucible Theatre in Sheffield will remain the home of the World Championship, with all its thrills, until the same date. Incidentally, by that time, Stephen Hendry will have reached the ripe old age of 27!

Yes, the future seems assured. Certainly, television has put the World Championship equal to, if not above, Wimbledon or The Derby, as a popular sporting event. TV has also given us those memories that for many would have held no interest a mere decade ago. How can we forget that famous night when a record eighteen and a half million people sat spellbound in the early hours, to watch Dennis Taylor sink the final black against Steve Davis and take the title. Then there was the picture of elation on the face of Cliff Thorburn as he knelt by the table when the last black dropped to record his championship maximum break in 1983. Memories could fill this book – John Ireland's caricatures will bring them all back to you.

RECENT WORLD CHAMPIONS

The 'interesting' Steve Davis is a professional to his fingertips. As a Thursday's child he had far to go, and proved it at an early age. He has had many 'firsts', such as the first maximum break on television, and becoming the first millionaire snooker player. The latter is a major goal of many people, but it really doesn't bother Steve – his true goal is perfection at the game he loves. Like the athlete struggling to take a second off his best time, so Steve strives for absolute accuracy in every stroke he plays.

He is a very private person, a gentleman both on and away from the table. During a tournament you will not see Steve 'hanging around' – he's either practising or reading a book in his dressing room. Between shows (or sessions) he can be seen lolling around in jeans and trainers, but 'on duty' he is immaculate in dress and behaviour. Don't get the wrong impression, when the job is done, the World's No. 1 can be one of the boys – full of laughter, gags, and 'Let's have another one!'

I well remember the first occasion the name Steve Davis was to be inscribed on the coveted World Championship trophy. We celebrated into the early hours whilst Steve lay on a couch, clutching the trophy and joining in the laughter. Then he just fell asleep amid all the hilarity. Perhaps that sums him up!

Born of a close-knit working-class family in Plumstead, South-east London, it was his Dad, Bill, who introduced and encouraged Steve to the billiards table. Still today Bill, who accompanies his son everywhere, will rebuke a fault, but in a fatherly way – his son is a big boy now!

Steve Davis

Dreams do come true, but not very often; I mean the sort of fairy tale that the world enjoys. Such was the case with Terry Griffiths. Having turned professional he entered his first tournament, the World Professional Snooker Championship. Before a capacity-packed Crucible Theatre audience and millions more on TV he got the better of Australia's Eddie Charlton, 19-17 in the semi-final, and made that classic remark, 'I'm in the final now, you know!!' Beating Dennis Taylor 24-16 in the final, his first professional tournament had made him World Champion and changed his life.

Before fame struck, Terry had been a postman, insurance agent and bus conductor. Although well known in his native Llanelli, little was known about him elsewhere until he won the All England Amateur Championship in 1977. He had won the Welsh Amateur in '75 but gained more prominence by taking the All England title for the second consecutive time in 1978.

A cueman with a delightful smooth flowing action, Terry practises incessantly. He is particular about his dress, always immaculate, and conducts himself as a gentleman at all times. He likes a cigarette but rarely drinks, preferring a pot of tea. He remains a modest man through his gentle charm and good manners. He still lives in his beloved Llanelli with his wife Annette and their two children, Wayne and Darren. Home is very important to Terry Griffiths. Never admitting to being a businessman, he and Annette have created their own snooker club in the town. I must go there, I hear tell it radiates the essence of its owners.

———————————◆———————————

Terry Griffiths

Alex Higgins is controversial, self-destructive, unpredictable, sometimes aggressive and can be extremely pleasant. He has an undeniable talent, and love him or hate him there has never been a better box-office draw. He first hit the headlines back in 1972 by winning the world title at his first attempt. Never out of the headlines, he took the title again ten years later.

Alex had to survive in a tough district in Belfast and in snooker he found success. He had hopes of becoming a jockey but it didn't work out. His quick thinking gave him a natural flair for the game and he would play for hours on end. He is completely self-taught, his style in absolute contrast to Steve Davis's. He is a rebel and hasn't too much time for the establishment. He makes no attempt to conceal pathos or dejection in defeat.

Away from the billiards table, Alex is a bit of a loner. He finds comfort in the bar, whether it be pub, club or theatre; he has tried his hand at golf, but no matter what interest attracts him he soon returns to what he found success in – playing snooker – and he will readily go anywhere in the world to do that.

Alex Higgins

Joe Johnson captured the hearts and admiration of millions when he won the World Professional title in 1986. The television cameras portrayed the lad from Bradford for exactly what he is – a happy-go-lucky chap, sincere as the day is long, and enjoying the game he loves, completely unperturbed by the success surrounding him. Those in the game knew it was no fluke, as he proved the following year, but the masses of armchair viewers were unaware he was World Amateur finalist before turning professional in 1979.

As children, home for Joe and his sister was Bradford Moor Liberal Club, where Mum and Dad were stewards. Dad was also captain of the club's snooker team. As the last member left the club Joe would creep downstairs for practice; he made the team quickly and went on to be a three-time winner of the Yorkshire Championship. Those amateur days remain a fond memory, for Dad took him everywhere to enhance his play and experience.

Joe left school at the age of 15 and took a course training to be a motor mechanic. It didn't last – in two years he never got inside a car. He had jobs with a haulage firm and the Gas Board but the call of the green baize, and the support of Mum and Dad, was overwhelming. Today the world's his oyster, his fame has spread to the far corners of the earth, but he still remains the lad from Bradford. Within a busy life he keeps weekends free whenever possible to share with wife Terryll and the family of four boys and two girls (four children are Joe's by a previous marriage). He is happiest when taking the kids to the local fair or circus – or just a romp in the park.

He endeavours to play golf, but says he does it badly, likes a smoke and the occasional pint, but is no gambler. He has a long-standing (12 years) rendezvous with a few pals at the local club, and when time permits will do a guest spot, singing with a group of boys known as Made in Japan.

Joe Johnson

Ray Reardon was something special when he arrived on the snooker scene in the early Seventies. Like many 14-year-old Welsh lads he had gone down the pits but found an escape through the game – he was eager to prove himself a champion. His father and uncles, like most miners, were addicted to snooker and every spare minute was spent at the Tredegar Miners' Institute. Ray was a natural from the start, and won the Welsh Amateur Championship before he was 18. The family moved to Stoke-on-Trent and Ray joined the Constabulary. Forsaking the 'blue' for more colours, he became a professional in 1967 via a number of amateur titles. His professional career is well documented, including no less than six world titles.

     Ray is a complete extrovert and the game's great ambassador. He has a tremendous communication with fans and friends alike. He is as much at home on the golf course as he is on the billiards table, and has an acute brain for business. Fond of a 'tiddly' or two when the show is over, his sociable nature enhances the demand for his services and Ray will travel anywhere he's needed. Having toured the world several times, his ready smile and twinkling eyes have helped lay the ground for today's worldwide circuit, and amid all his other commitments he still finds time to be President of the World Professional Billiards and Snooker Association.

Ray Reardon

A late entrant into the professional ranks, John Spencer, like his contemporary Ray Reardon, had turned 30 when he made the bold step. And it was a bold step, for in those days, the early Seventies, there was little in the way of tournament snooker. 'Pot Black' had just arrived on our TV screens and only a handful of players made up the membership of the Professional Players Association. Spencer and Reardon dominated the scene for the next decade, John winning the world title three times and Ray six. During those ten years several sponsorships appeared and John Spencer won all of them.

A great potter, tactician and breakbuilder, he also has a wicked sense of humour. This developed with the years and he became the game's No. 1 leg-puller. No-one is safe from the Spencer wind-up. He was to present a tray of cut glass to the Sports Chief of the BBC. As he handed the gift over he dropped the tray to the stone floor – imagine the aghast looks – then slipped out and came back with the real thing, now beaming that wicked smile. I leave you to guess what goes on in the commentary box, where he is now part of our team.

Born in Radcliffe just outside Manchester, John Spencer worked in a bookmaker's office on leaving school, and that interest stays with him. He loves a gamble, and I suggest you be very wary if you find yourself in competition with him, whether it be golf, cards or tiddlywinks.

John Spencer

At the age of 10, Dennis Taylor spent hours watching his father and older brother Martin play snooker. By the time he was 14 he could beat them both. Leaving home in Coalisland, Co. Tyrone at 17 to join an aunt in Lancashire, he worked long hours in a paper mill, but found a billiards table at every spare opportunity. He is living proof of the tough road to the top in snooker, for it took Dennis 12 years to gain a significant win – the Rothman's Grand Prix in 1984. He climaxed this the following spring with that epic World Final against Steve Davis. Dennis took the final black, the title, and a record 18 million TV viewers watched into the early hours.

This Irishman is one of the most popular characters in the game – full of fun and funny stories. When not playing snooker he loves nothing better than being on a golf course. During a round with a pal one day, his pal fainted. Quipped Dennis, 'If that's a stroke, put it on his card!' His ready wit and laughing Irish eyes bring many demands for TV quiz shows and after-dinner speaking. A proud family man, he and wife Pat have three children, Denise, Damian and Brendan; home is important to him – he still lives in Lancashire.

Whilst Dennis Taylor may never again win that world title, his winning personality will always ensure a multitude of friends.

Dennis Taylor

'The Grinder', as he is affectionately known by all – in particular by Terry Griffiths after their second-round final session in the 1983 Championship took 9 hours, finishing around 4 am, with Cliff Thorburn taking the final frame to win 13-12. The toughest match player anyone can meet is also a very nice guy. From Toronto, Canada, Cliff Thorburn began playing in a local pool room and learnt the hard way. He would take any job to get a few dollars with which to gamble on himself at pool, and in this way he hustled his way across Canada and North America.

His vast experience paid off. He dominated the Canadian snooker championships, became their No. 1 star and came to England in 1973 for more experience. The game was different, with smaller pockets and heavier balls, and it took him to 1980 before he realised his ambition to become World Champion. Cliff climaxed this in 1983 by making the maximum 147, the first and only player (so far) to do so in a World Championship.

With his wife Barbara, a former Canadian sprinter, and their two young children, the family have taken up residence on this side of the Atlantic. Cliff is a more than useful golfer (with a two/three handicap) and enjoys a party – he poured a bottle of Champagne over me when the Canadians won the World Teams in 1982, and has a terrific sense of humour. A gentleman at all times, he is welcomed to any shores – and he's been to most of them.

Cliff Thorburn

It has always been said that the billiards room was strictly a
male domain. This is not true. Cleopatra played billards, Queen
Victoria was among the first to have rubber cushions fitted to
her table at Windsor Castle, and it is said that Mary, Queen of
Scots pleaded for her billiards table when in captivity.

It is true that most billiard rooms in the pubs and clubs
of Great Britain have over the years been restricted to 'men only'.
This barrier to a large extent has now been broken down. Today
there are 'mixed' tournaments for world titles.

The Women's Billiards Association was first formed in
1931 by a group of enthusiastic women cueists, and was affiliated
to the governing body, the Billiards and Snooker Control
Council. They set up women's billiards circles in the major towns
of the UK, and now the organised girls of the Eighties have
tournaments in Australia, Canada, Holland and Belgium, and
sponsorships totalling thousands. The Ladies' World
Championship alone carries £10,000 prize money – a great step
forward! They need more national exposure, particularly on
television, and are working hard to win it.

World champion of the ladies is a young go-getter from
Peacehaven, Sussex – Alison Fisher. She first held the title in
1985, and has only missed out once since then in '87, when
another promising young lady, Ann Marie Farren, made her
intentions clear by taking the crown. Alison had dominated
ladies' snooker over the past four or five years, and today
regularly competes in male tournaments. She is closely
challenged by a twenty-year-old from Dorset, Stacey Hillyard.
Like many of today's young players, both female and male,
Stacey became fascinated with snooker through TV. Her Mum
and Dad bought her a small table when she was 12, now she
practises five hours a day and is ranked No. 2 in the world. The
Ladies' Association regard themselves as merely 'players', but
Alison, Stacey and Anne Marie are hoping to gain membership
of the male profession. 'Turn over, Cleopatra!'

Alison Fisher

THE CONTENDERS

Australian Eddie Charlton is a fitness fanatic. He runs anything
between five and ten miles every morning before breakfast,
takes health tablets every day and carries his own specially
prepared cereals wherever his travels take him. He was born in
Swansea, NSW and was encouraged to play billiards by his
grandfather who owned a billiard club. At the age of nine,
however, he favoured other school sports, interests which stayed
with him into manhood.

He became proficient to professional standards at soccer
and tennis, was a member of the crew to win the Australian
Surfing Championship, had a short professional boxing career,
and collected a good string of victories at speed roller skating.
Grandfather, however, was persistent to the end, and Eddie
Charlton found world recognition at billiards and snooker. He
was for twenty years Australia's Professional Snooker
Champion.

Away from the table, Eddie eats, drinks and sleeps
business – the phone is never far from his ear. He is a non-smoker
but enjoys a few whiskies in those odd moments of relaxation.
He is a fussy dresser and has an extremely tidy mind. Everything
has to be in its right place and to watch him pack his suitcase is
an education.

The apple of his eye is his young son, Andrew, by his
second marriage, the two sons and a daughter of his first
marriage now having grown up. The busy schedule of
tournaments this side of the world keep the Charltons in
England for up to nine months out of the year, but Eddie's
business interests 'down under' are alluring.

Eddie Charlton

Tony Drago is a young man in a hurry – a world-beater each time he comes to the table. His quick-fire attack at almost every shot confronting him, has caught the imagination of the television millions; but it has also cost him vital frames. None more so than when a missed yellow against Steve Davis robbed him of a semi-final place in the UK Open Championship last year.

Tony first came to Great Britain in 1982 with the financial help of friends. Life had been tough back home in Valletta, Malta where he was born and brought up with two sisters and two brothers. He had a language problem when he arrived and for a while suffered homesickness. The monthly trips back to Malta have dwindled a little in the last couple of years. His rise up the ranking list and his exciting style have brought an air of confidence both on and off the table.

A tall boy, he is over six feet and takes after his Dad who is a policeman in Valletta and started playing snooker at the very young age of six. When he left school Tony had no thought of getting a job, he could earn what he needed on the snooker table. Still today his only thoughts and conversation are about the frame he has just played, or the one he is about to play. He is a non-smoker and non-drinker, and has no other hobbies.

Having turned professional in 1985, he has set his sights on making a big name as Malta's only pro star. If maturity is kind, he can do just that.

Tony Drago

The quiet, unasssuming and reserved Neal Foulds is the one snooker star who prefers to shun publicity. A loner, who likes to pick his own friends, in particular those in less well-off circumstances than himself. Even through school, the robust type was not for him. He has one constant companion, his father Geoff. They are inseparable.

Geoff, a knowledgeable player and coach, is also a protective father who joined the professional ranks in 1981 and has largely surrendered his own professional career to encourage, advise and guide his son. They are the only father and son players in the profession.

Neal showed great promise as a youngster, mainly due to his father's influence, and got his first taste of the television cameras when only 17 in 'Junior Pot Black'. He was London Junior Champion at 16 and won the British Junior Championship in 1982 at 19. In July 1983 he became a professional and today is ranked among the world's top eight.

His reticent manner may be partly due to the fact that since childhood he has suffered to a high degree with eyesight problems. Specs were forsaken in favour of contact lenses which today are almost as important as his cue. With additional personal problems and a slight heart complaint his game has recently suffered, but he has the ambition and the temperament to overcome all.

Away from the snooker room he loves nothing better than to watch cricket – a day spent at Lord's is peace and heaven. In complete contrast he loves the thrills and excitement of greyhound racing. Again this is Dad's influence, for since boyhood father and son have owned and raced greyhounds. Not surprisingly, Wembley Stadium is just around the corner from home.

With his younger sister, Susie, and his even younger son Darren to back him up, and a caring Mum and Dad, the future for Neal Foulds is assured.

Neal Foulds

The Franciscos are a billiards and snooker-playing family. Dad, Manuel, was Portuguese and moved to Capetown, South Africa before any family arrived. A good player himself, he bought a cafe and had a billiards table installed at the rear of the premises. Their first son, Manuel, made good use of that table and became one of South Africa's best snooker players. It was natural that Silvino should follow in his elder brother's footsteps, and he did so in style winning the SA Amateur Championship five times.

Turning professional in 1978, he came to England in 1982 and has settled in Chesterfield with his wife Denise and their young family. The odd thing is, Denise is an English girl who moved to South Africa with her family. Then, having married Silvino she settled in England, leaving both their families in Capetown! 'It's a long way to visit Mum and Dad,' she says. To add to the confusion, Silvino's nephew Peter has also moved to the UK and is now chasing his uncle for snooker honours.

Silvino himself loves sport. He follows bowls, boxing and football on TV, and plays squash to keep fit, but in England is robbed of his favourite pastime, scuba-diving. Fishing is also high on his list, and if our climate would allow, he would lie in the sun all day. A non-smoker and very much a family man, he rarely appears on the party scene.

At the snooker table he is a difficult opponent with a potting ability second to none when in form. He won the British Open in 1985 and the South African Professional Championship the following year, but controversies in the past two years have disturbed his concentration. He has been in the world's top ten, and my guess is he will be back there in the not-too-distant future.

Silvino Francisco

A polite and pleasant young man with an assured future is Mike Hallett, whose charm endears him to all who meet him. Dad, a building contractor in Grimsby (Mike lost his mum in 1970), played snooker in the Army for enjoyment, and he, together with life-long friend Cliff Ayers, are responsible for his upbringing and dedication to his chosen career. Sister Ann and the family are his most ardent fans. In earlier days aunts and uncles would telephone one another with his achievements, whether good or bad.

Like most of today's young stars, Mike took to snooker through watching 'Pot Black'. At the age of 10, Dad bought him a small table. He played truant from school and for hours would silently watch others much older in the billiard hall; then went home to practise what he had seen. He has never had a lesson at the game.

On leaving school he joined the Customs agents of a shipping company, looking after cargo ships entering and leaving his native Grimsby. But snooker ruled and at 17 he was offered a sponsorship – more fatherly than businesslike – which advanced him to professionalism in 1979.

Mike Hallett drifted through his early professional years, searching for a guiding hand, a mentor. Over five or six years he gained the odd success, but was learning all the time. Then bingo! The Scottish businessman, Ian Doyle, who has groomed Stephen Hendry to stardom, signed him up, and in a short time he has matured and succeeded.

A non-smoker, he is fond of travel and expensive clothes. He likes fast cars and enjoys rallying. He plays golf, and recently has taken up ten pin bowling. His new home in Cleethorpes, shared with Janet, houses a billiard room. Mike is here to stay.

Mike Hallett

Stephen Hendry was only 14 years old when he made his début on television – in 'Junior Pot Black 1983'. I well remember his Dad, Gordon, bringing him to Pebble Mill Studios, Birmingham for that recording – a 4ft 9in lad from Scotland, happy and proud to be wearing his first pair of long trousers. Now six years on he is being acclaimed as a potential World Snooker Champion and the second millionaire snooker star.

Young Stephen got hooked on the game through watching 'Pot Black'. His parents bought him a small table for Christmas and he's never looked back, having won several major titles both at home and abroad. Still a shy boy but now over 6 feet tall, he matures in stature and performance with each passing day. Ably managed and guided by Scottish businessman Ian Doyle, this baby of the snooker profession has a very bright future indeed.

Time has passed quickly for young Stephen with major tournaments both in the UK and overseas claiming his appearance – he's already the world's number two star. In the last 12 months he has taken up golf as a relaxation, and I understand he is doing pretty well there as well. Watch out, Sandy Lyle, there's another Scotsman on the green.

By the way, the only Scot to win the world title was Walter Donaldson back in 1950. He defeated Fred Davis 51-46 in the final. They were marathons in those days!

Stephen Hendry

Tall, dark and handsome – a firm favourite with the fair sex –
Tony Knowles was born in Bolton in 1955, one of three brothers.
Attracted to snooker at the age of nine, he got his first taste of
success at 16 by twice winning the British Junior Championship,
firstly in 1972, and again in '74. He waited, however, until 1980
before taking the plunge into the professional ranks. His big
moment came in the first round of the 1982 World Championship
when he beat Steve Davis 10 frames to 1. Tony had arrived! He's
been in the top ten ever since.

He can remember, and will 'talk over', almost every shot
he has played in any match for days afterwards. The inquest is a
form of practice to him, he learns by his mistakes. Tony also has
strong views on the whys and wherefores of the game, but has no
aspirations for a seat within the administration. He has
overcome adverse publicity and now strives for recognition at the
very top, and is capable of doing so.

At home, his delightful cottage overlooks his own lake,
on which sits his speed-boat. One way he keeps fit is water-
skiing, and he also plays squash, tennis and golf. Another side of
this complex character is his domesticity – he loves cooking and
is very good at it. His Snooker Club and Night Spot is left in the
hands of Dad (a former club steward) and his brother Michael;
and Tony's favourite escape is his villa in Tenerife where he soaks
up the sun at all available opportunities. Although the world
title has so far eluded him, he has many other titles in his chosen
profession. One thing is for sure – Tony Knowles's life-style is
second to none.

Tony Knowles

The only child of a Sicilian father and an Italian mother, Tony Meo was born in London and is proud to say he is British. His parents came to England, met and married, and set up a restaurant in Marylebone. On Tony's arrival they moved south to Tooting and when he started school he found a mate by the name of Jimmy White. The families lived in adjoining streets and just around the corner was a billiard hall. That was just the beginning.

It is fair to say, however, that Tony gained a little more from school than Jimmy. His days of truancy started at 13, whereas Jimmy had been escaping to the billiard hall from the age of 11. Learning in school is an important and concerning time in a boy's life, and for Tony it was made more so by the death of his father. Mum (in Tony's words, a real grafter) set to work to feed and clothe herself and young son, which gave the young Meo more time for practice in the billiard hall. His achievements proved more successful than his schooling.

He did try a job, as a sort of dispatch clerk with an architectural ironmongers. It paid £20 a week in arrears, and he knew he could earn that at snooker in one hour, so asked for his week's wages to be sent on!

His professional career started in 1979 after making his way to the final of the Canadian Open. Two years later he won the Australian Masters in Sydney. In 1985 he won it again. Victories in the Doubles (with Steve Davis) in Thailand, and more recently the British Open have kept Tony Meo in the headlines.

An emotional and courteous young man he is a snappy dresser, who loves a day at the races and listening to jazz. His house in Surrey is shared with wife Denise and their three children Tina, Tony and Sonny. They are a happy family surrounded by cosiness.

Tony Meo

Graham Miles was born in Birmingham during the last war, the son of a city tram driver. Both Mum and Dad had one child by previous marriages, so Graham found himself with a sister and brother neither of whom had the same parents as he did. The three have been life-long pals. His stepbrother became a very good snooker player, but Graham much preferred table tennis at which he excelled. Looking for county honours, he needed plenty of practice but grew impatient waiting for his turn on the table at his Youth Club. Fed up one day, he tried his hand on the billiards table. He was twelve then, and, as they say, the rest is history.

On leaving school, he became an apprentice in engineering and gained his City and Guilds Certificate. Through to his mid-twenties he tried various jobs – selling hot dogs, working on building sites, even selling greengrocery by travelling van – but none gave the satisfaction the billiard table offered. Having won most local snooker tournaments, Graham became Midland Amateur Champion, and in 1969 turned professional.

Invited into 'Pot Black' as a substitute in 1974, he won it – and to prove it was no fluke he won it again the following year. In Australia he won their Television Masters Tournament, and still takes pride in the trophy he won to become the first State Express champion. He owns a highly successful club in Crewe and has a part-interest in another in Birmingham. Graham is the first to admit his clubs have taken the place of his world travels.

Graham and his wife Heather (she's also a Brummy!) have never moved from their roots. Their son Tony shares Dad's love of sport, but Miles Senior is an armchair sportsman – he prefers it on television. Fond of reading, he also enjoys a game of chess. He likes a drink and a smoke, but rarely goes to parties; when he does, he's usually the clown. Heather thinks he's eccentric, and is convinced he will arrive late for his own funeral. Let's hope that day is a long way off.

Graham Miles

On leaving school, Doug Mountjoy followed his father into the pits but, like many other Welsh lads it was the billiards club that claimed his attention. Doug had played snooker for fun as a boy in his birthplace of Tir-y-berth in Glamorgan, and now he had started work was anxious to show his mates that his childhood fun was no waste of time. He soon became Welsh Amateur Champion. He won the World Amateur title twice, the second time in Jonannesburg, and then turned pro. The only title that eludes him as a professional is the world crown and he acknowledges that time is running out on that.

A modest man who enjoys his nightly pint, Doug thinks of nothing but snooker. He has no ambitions to become a business tycoon, preferring when not playing to visit the bar with pals and talk about the game over a drink and a smoke. He does allow himself the odd game of golf, but rarely does he leave his beloved Wales except for snooker.

Home is very important to him. Once asked by a reporter to name his favourite holiday spot, Doug replied, 'Home.' He shares a delightful house with his wife Yvonne and their two children, Yvette and Andrew. Maybe they have things just right – surrounded by everything they love most.

Doug Mountjoy

The young New Zealander Dene O'Kane first came to England as an amateur in 1981, having won the NZ Amateur Snooker Championship the previous year. Oddly enough it was 1981 that saw the passing of the great New Zealand billiards player Clark McConachy, at the age of 85. Dene has a big responsibility in his chosen vocation for there has only ever been one world-class professional from his country.

His début on this side of the world was in the first series of BBC's 'Junior Pot Black' in 1981 and he gave a good account of himself by reaching the final. It is interesting to note that also appearing in that first series were Neal Foulds, Mark Bennett, John Parrott and Dean Reynolds – the latter beating O'Kane in the final. 'Junior Pot Black' was designed for promising young amateurs and it bore fruit – add the names Paddy Browne and Stephen Hendry and you have seven of today's established young professionals.

Dene O'Kane started playing as a child with a broomhandle and ping-pong balls on a rug in front of the fire – he had been watching Ray Reardon on 'Pot Black' on TV. Then with the help of instructional books by Joe Davis he graduated to the billiard tables at the YMCA where his Dad was manager. To please Mum he started work as a clerk in a shipping company, but it lasted only nine months. The call of the billiards hall was too great.

His visit to our shores has now lasted eight years – he turned professional here in 1984. Endeavouring to return home twice each year, he finds each visit more emotional. The hellos and goodbyes to those near to him cause a lot of mental upheaval, particularly where a certain young lady is concerned. His dreams lie in the countryside of Cheshire, a far cry from his favourite hobby of skin-diving.

One thing is for sure: whether he becomes World Champion or not, he will finally settle back in New Zealand. Dene is very patriotic and if he admitted his inner feelings you would find a homesick young man.

Dene O'Kane

Undoubtedly a character of the future is John Parrott. He has a great sense of humour – he's heard, enjoyed and used all the gags: 'Who's a pretty boy then', 'He's a cagey character', 'Falling off his perch', etc., etc. His ready Liverpudlian wit is equal to any smart quip delivered from the tongues of those who attempt to be clever at his expense.

A tall young man with a pleasing personality, good looks, and attentive to his dress, John has recently married his sweetheart of five years, Karen, also a Liverpudlian. He is an only son, his Mum and Dad having divorced when he was quite young. It was Dad, Alan, who encouraged him in conjunction with his life-long friend and manager, Phil Miller.

He left school with six 'O' levels and has always loved sport. He is a keen follower of Everton and Liverpool from childhood, and first took up crown green bowls; he became a six-handicap golfer and today finds relaxation and enjoyment in horse racing.

Although he is only 25 years old, snooker has already taken him all over the world since he turned professional in 1983 – from Australia and Hong Kong to China (where he won the Kent Cup) and Thailand; through Canada and Europe, where in Deauville in 1989 he registered his first big ranking tournament win in the European Open.

It was back in 1981, when only 17, that John first came to prominence. He was invited on 'Junior Pot Black' and won two of the three series recorded for TV. He has a unique record in the Pontin Festival of Snooker: as an amateur he won the Junior and Open tournaments, and as a professional he has taken both Open and Pro titles – four successes no other player has achieved.

This pleasant young man will grace our TV screens for a long time to come, bringing enjoyment to his fans as his attractive play reaches for greater glories.

John Parrott

We might never have seen Dean Reynolds walk those steps into the arena of the Crucible Theatre, Sheffield, for it was a toss-up whether he chose football or snooker as his career. At school the favours fell heavily on the left wing, where he showed such promise that Lincoln City were interested. Snooker, however, won the toss and it was Dad who threw the coin up.

You see, Dad, a welder, was a pretty good snooker player, and won nearly all the local tournaments in the area around Grimsby where Dean, his brother and sister were brought up. As eldest of the three children Dean often accompanied Dad to his matches, and for six or seven years waited anxiously for the table lights to go out after the match so that he could grab a cue and knock the balls around. By the time he was 16 he was good enough to win the Lincs and South Humberside Junior Championship.

Two years later, in 1981, in company with other familiar names in today's professional world – Parrott, Foulds, O'Kane – he was invited to play in the first televised series of 'Junior Pot Black', and fought his way to the final. His opponent in that final was the young New Zealander, Dene O'Kane. Reynolds proved the stronger and carried off the honours. He turned professional that same year, and in that tough world is still struggling for his goal of a big title.

A bit of a loner, Dean loves nothing more than relaxing on the banks of a river, freshwater fishing. He plays golf with a handicap of 18 and considers cars are merely a way of getting from A to B. His feet are firmly on the ground, and with Joanne has found a new home where they look forward to the responsibility of a family.

Dean Reynolds

The third and youngest of the Canadian stars to move to the UK was Kirk Stevens. Cliff Thorburn (Kirk's idol) and Bill Werbeniuk had already moved across the Atlantic to get experience in the match-play of our more buoyant snooker scene. Kirk had won the Canadian Open Championship in 1978, turned professional in 1979 and was anxious to prove himself.

He was born in Toronto in 1958 and his childhood was not easy. His mother and father were divorced when he was seven, and several young years were used up in a parental tug-of-war. Kirk has always been very close to his Dad, who has given him life-long inspiration. School was of no interest to him, but sport was. A cousin was a professional ice-hockey player, and Kirk took to baseball. He also enjoyed swimming and golf. It was Dad who encouraged him, at the age of 10, to play snooker.

The attraction of his early appearances here were not solely his excellent potting. He wore white suits which added more glamour to his flamboyant style and quickly gave him that pop idol image. His play took him to the semi-finals of the World Championship in 1980 and the final of the New Zealand Masters in 1984. Undoubtedly his greatest thrill was his magnificent maximum of 147 on TV against Jimmy White in the 1984 Benson and Hedges Masters. It earned him £10,000.

Through the traumas of life Kirk has remained a quiet, polite and charming young man, and is one of snooker's eligible bachelors. The past couple or so years have brought further problems when he admitted using drugs. His strength of character, and his family, have overcome those difficulties, and the unassuming and likeable young Canadian is fighting the trail once again.

Kirk Stevens

Willie Thorne is the 'Maximum Man' who has never really matured. Mum and Dad were highly successful publicans in Leicester, and although parted a long time ago, remain the best of pals. The adoration for their middle son (Willie has two brothers) is as strong today as when he won the Boys' Billiards and Snooker Championship back in 1970.

In practice and among friends, Willie is brilliantly outstanding, but in the loneliness of the big-match arena his talent ebbs and flows. His ability for building breaks is second to none. With more maximum clearances (hence his nickname) to his credit than any other player, only once has his mass of fans seen his prowess in tournament play – the magic 147 in the 1987 UK Championship.

Turning professional in 1975 so that he could participate in that year's 'Pot Black' series, Willie has claimed titles at home and abroad, and keeps up an all-round interest in sport. On the business side he owns five snooker clubs, administered by Mum and his two brothers, Malcolm and Robert.

Although 'one of the lads', family life is important to him. He and his wife Fiona have three children with twins, Tristian and Kieran arriving first. Image is also high on Willie's priorities – his Mercedes has the personal number plate A 147 PRO.

Away from the smoke of the billiards room (he is a non-smoker and almost non-drinker), the Maximum Man enjoys fishing, loves football (his best man was Gary Lineker) and is not unknown in the world of horse racing. His golf handicap is 19. Always sociable and easy going, the polished bald head of Willie Thorne will reflect all that is gentlemanly in snooker.

Willie Thorne

Mention 'Paint your Wagon' and one immediately thinks of 'Wanderin' Star', a title so easily befitting Bill Werbeniuk. Born in Winnipeg in January 1947, 'Big Bill', as he is affectionately known, is a happy-go-lucky character, scaling around 20 stone and with a sense of humour to match his size. He always has a big smile and a ready wit, and 'was' as popular as the song that befits him, and that reached Number 1. I say 'was' sadly, for it appears he has returned to Vancouver, where the family finally settled, and Mum still lives, being no longer a member of the snooker profession.

His father died when Bill was in his early teens, but not before passing on a little education from his own life-style. Dad was a gambler and hustler around the towns and clubs of Canada. Bill was quick to learn on his occasional trips with father and soon became proficient at both snooker and pool. His education included cards, and today he is one of the top card players in Canada. Another favourite is backgammon, at which Bill will spend enough days to fill a week.

The flamboyant Canadian won the North American Open Championship in his twenties, and still holds that title for the tournament has never been played since. He was the first of the four top Canadians to move to England to enhance his career, but his great prowess never brought him the title he longed for. I am happy to say I held the microphone in commentary when he won the New Zealand Masters in Auckland in 1983.

Bill's love of freedom and travel is well suited to the circuits of snooker and pool – let's hope the likeable Wanderin' Star will one day return.

Bill Werbeniuk

The very essence of the true snooker player can be found nowhere better than in the life of Jimmy White. Playing truant from school to such a degree, his headmaster finally capitulated, and allowed his pupil afternoon absence in order to play snooker at the local billiard hall. His education suffered, but those afternoons were the stepping stones to world stardom.

At the tender age of 16 he was All England Amateur Snooker Champion and within two years had become the youngest-ever World Amateur Champion. He turned professional when only 19 in 1981, and carried off the titles in his first two pro tournaments – in Scotland and Ireland.

Jimmy's natural ability on a billiards table is the envy of many top players. It can be said, however, that his flamboyant style has given away as many frames as some players have ever won. In maturity he is more cautious; after all he is now 27 years of age, and fully intends staying at the top.

Away from the competition arenas, Jimmy's life-style is similar to his snooker – he will have a go at anything. He enjoys life to the full; is popular with friends and fans the world over, and takes his responsibilities seriously. Jimmy is married and has two lovely children.

With three brothers and a sister, home has always been a loving one, and on the tournament circuit always his greatest fan and supporter there with him is his Dad, Tommy White, a builder and decorator from Tooting, South London.

Jimmy White had no silver spoon when he came into this world in 1962, but when he finally bows out there will be an abundance of silver trophies.

Jimmy White

One of the few players who has never experienced hardship, Rex Williams and brother Ken enjoyed the best of everything from childhood. Their Dad, 'Bill', was managing director of a highly successful printing works in Blackheath, Birmingham, and he was also a very strict disciplinarian. The boys grew up surrounded by business and Rex always had the happy knack of twisting his father's little finger.

At the age of 13 he started playing billiards and snooker and almost immediately won the Midland Boys' Championship. By the time he was 17 he had become English Amateur Snooker Champion. He turned professional in 1952 and on a tour of South Africa in '65 made the second world record maximum break of 147 (Joe Davis made the first, ten years earlier). In 1968 he travelled to New Zealand to win the Worlds Billiards title. Over the years the three-ball game has given him most pleasure.

Rex's business upbringing never left him. With brother Ken, he went into billiards and pool table manufacture and cue-making. As Chairman of the WPBSA he guided the Association through difficult times. For relaxation he turned to golf, and bowls at which he is county standard. Married with two grown-up daughters, Rex still enjoys the best in life; a lovely home complete with swimming pool in the Worcestershire countryside, a host of influential friends and a bottle of Champagne always available in the ice bucket.

Rex Williams

Cliff Wilson went to school in Tredegar with another young Welsh lad who was to make his name in the world of snooker – none other than Ray Reardon. As young amateurs, they had many battles on the billiards table. Cliff has had two successful careers in the game – most have difficulty in achieving one! He won the British Boys' Junior Championship for two consecutive years, 1952 and 1953, before the age of twenty, became Welsh Amateur Champion in 1956 and promptly gave up the game. Twenty-one years later he picked up his cue again; recaptured the Welsh title and travelled to Malta in 1978 to win the World Amateur Championship, defeating another of today's big names, Joe Johnson, in the final.

His withdrawal from snooker was mainly due to eyesight problems which had troubled him from childhood. He took up a job in a South Wales steelworks where he was an active shop steward; and with his wife Val (he calls her 'The Dragon', affectionately) helped bring up their four sons. He turned professional in 1979 after winning the world amateur title.

As portrayed in his snooker, Cliff is a happy-go-lucky guy – full of fun, and laughing and cracking gags from breakfast to bedtime. His cavalier approach makes him a crowd pleaser, but he is not afraid to speak his mind when needs be. A favourite hobby is the gee-gees, he likes a bet and can often be seen at the races. He enjoys a drink and a smoke, and although carrying a little weight likes nothing better than a restaurant with good home cooking. Now a silver-haired grandfather, he appreciates and enjoys the success of his Indian Summer – he's in the top 16 in the world and as such has a full list of engagements.

Cliff Wilson

John Virgo has come a very long way since his childhood days in Salford, Lancashire, where he was born. Money was not too readily available in those days, and on leaving school John got himself a job as an invoice clerk to pay his Mum a few bob for his keep. He would hustle around the clubs in the area to get the luxuries he felt he needed, like a smoke and a bet. His second love has always been horse racing. Today as Chairman of the World Professional Billiards and Snooker Association, he steers the destiny of millions of pounds and the development of worldwide operations.

He was a Junior Champion of Great Britain and turned professional in 1976. Three years later he won the UK Professional title, and in 1980 went to India to win an international championship. The big tournaments have escaped him, but his presence is felt in most of them. Through television, John has a huge following for his impressions of other players and is also a regular member of the BBC commentary team.

Offstage, he is the funniest of men, particularly when he has had a few, though you would never think so watching him in a match! He is a very caring person to all in the profession – I can personally vouch for that! He has realised his ambition to own racehorses, and is lucky enough to have a wife who efficiently runs his business affairs and the lovely home they share with their young family in Surrey.

John Virgo

THE REFEREES

As a top referee in the professional world of snooker, Alan Chamberlain is an unusual breed. He is no player and never had any aspirations to being part of the game. He was born in Market Harborough, the son of a factory production manager, and Dad's only interest was the odd frame whilst serving in the Auxiliary Fire Service during the war.

Alan was taught the piano as a child and it has stayed with him through life – for a while he was assistant organist at his Parish Church. His other hobby is classical music (he has a large collection), but he will tolerate ballet and light opera. He also sang with the Market Harborough Operatic Society.

From youth he yearned for the outdoor life and set his sights on selling. On leaving grammar school he found a job in the sales department of a Leicester haberdashery company but returned to his home town to work in a corset factory. Within 12 months he became secretary of a sports and social club and then found his forte in selling ladies' lingerie under the famous Gossard label. For 17 years he was his own boss as a self-employed agent throughout the East Midlands.

Refereeing snooker never entered his head until one day he went to see a match between Ray Reardon and John Spencer, and the 'third man' intrigued him. His interest stirred the thought that there was no active referee in the Leicester area; he studied the game until it became an obsession, he joined the Referees' Association and finally turned professional in 1983. After years of longing for the outdoor life he had come in out of the cold.

Although he rarely smiles on-screen, Alan enjoys a party, but readily admits he's no night owl. He likes eating out and has recently acquired a taste for Indian food. Fond of travel, he gets great joy from driving his new sports car. Careful, Alan – one heart attack is enough!!

Alan Chamberlain

The 'Jolly Green Giant' is just one of the name tags given to referee Len Ganley. You could add 'The Laughing Ref', or 'Snooker's Sergeant Major' – his voice is authoritative, particularly if an audience becomes over-enthusiastic – and then again he is known as the 'Ball Crusher' (following his TV advert for a well known lager). Whichever tag you prefer, Len always has a cheerful smile, and a willingness to lend a hand at all times.

He was born in Lurgan, Northern Ireland on 27 April 1943, the seventh son of a seventh son. Castle Lane still holds loving memories for him, and on leaving school he became a chimney sweep, following the footsteps of his father and grandfather. He spent three and a half years cleaning the chimneys around Lurgan and then the family moved to Lisburn where Len became a bus conductor. When not conducting buses he learnt to play snooker.

He came to England in 1970 for a short holiday, and, willing to pay his way, found himself a job with a shoe manufacturer in Burton-on-Trent, where he still lives. Snooker is prominent in the brewing town, and Len made his mark – winning the Burton League seven times and the Open twice. He remembered marking at the Lurgan Catholic Association when a mere child and was now doing so for his team-mates. The interest grew and he became a professional referee in 1979.

A strong family man, Len has four sons and two daughters and two grandchildren. He considers he has around 700 living relatives, and not surprisingly he is a great charity worker. When time permits he enjoys golf, bowls and swimming, but mostly he likes communication. The last time I saw him, he was talking in sign language to a young deaf and dumb snooker fan.

Len Ganley

Born in Dublin in 1928, John Smyth is an elder in today's band of professional referees. He became fascinated with snooker as a child by sneaking into the hall next to Mooneys pub where his father was manager. Dad was not interested in the billiards table and his brother was hooked on darts; a younger sister has no thought for either.

Leaving school at 16 with nothing particular in mind, he took a job as assistant barman at the golf club. It wasn't long before his fancies turned to dairy farming, but that finished with milk deliveries. He tried his hand at the greyhound kennels and then for two years became a stable lad with Mickey Burn at Phoenix Park Racecourse. Returning to his milk round for a couple of years, John decided the grass must be greener in London and (wait for it) got a job as a night doorkeeper at the Nurses Home for University College Hospital. John finally found his niche in 1950 as an Underground train driver where he stayed for 28 years, finishing as an instructor.

The job with London Transport gave him time to concentrate on his childhood love of snooker – he won the Transport Championship six times – and through his friendship with that grand old billiard marker, the late Frank Little, he took to refereeing and eventually turned professional in 1978 on his retirement from the 'underground movements'!

A family man with one son and three grandchildren, John Smyth has had little time for other sports except on TV. He finds relaxation in Country and Western music, and enjoys reading stories of the old Wild West. His early days in London were lonely ones, but snooker fulfilled his every dream.

John Smyth

The Devonshire brogue and familiar face of John Street are as much part of televised snooker as the players themselves. With distinguished grey hair combed straight back, and ruddy complexion, one would never suspect a weak child – suffering through boyhood with tuberculosis.

As a youngster John's first love was table tennis, at which he became very proficient; but his illness caused a 14-month spell in hospital and realisation struck home. The important years of his youth were impeded – even football and cricket had to be forgotten. Looking for a less energetic sport he chose snooker and joined a club run by Mrs Pulman, the mother of the famous John Pulman. In a short time he was playing in league snooker and became one of the local top ten players with regular breaks of 60 and 70.

John's refereeing started in those league matches, helping out his team-mates; and although not wholly interested he applied for and received a referee's certificate back in 1960 whilst endeavouring to find a job to suit his health. Finally settling as a district agent for Pearl Assurance (his job for 18 years), he found less time for playing, but was able to continue his interest in the game through refereeing. He became a professional referee in 1986.

Born and brought up in Exmouth, John Street has spent most of his life in Exeter where he still lives today with his wife Jean and their two daughters. Naturally he is fond of the sea and loves nothing better than fishing from his 22-foot cabin cruiser whenever time allows away from the artificial lights and the green baize.

As a professional referee he has found new strengths – it has changed his life. His articles in *Pot Black Magazine* bring forth a regular fan mail, and he travels the world over officiating at big tournaments as far afield as Helsinki and Monte Carlo. John enjoys his job, his travels, and his life of today.

John Street

You can't fail to recognise John Williams on your TV screen. His parting clutches his left ear and thin strands of hair sprawl over his head. His face has appeared over more years than many of today's players have been in the professional ranks. He was the 'middle one' of seven children, having three brothers and three sisters, and like many Welsh lads was weaned on billiards and snooker. Grandfather was English bar billiards champion and father Edward was a good player at both games. The mother of one of John's school pals ran a billiards club and his education started there.

On the academic side, he left school with seven 'O' levels and with training and night school gained qualifications in metallurgy. He joined the metal laboratory of British Steel, and finished his business life in the Civil Service as an executive officer in the Department of Employment.

His early attachment to snooker never left him, and although a useful league player he realised his limits and turned to refereeing. At heart he is an organiser and takes great pride in the detailed arrangements of an event. Back in 1974 it was John who worked out the playing format for almost 1,000 entrants as he helped me to initiate the Pontin Snooker Festival.

As the senior man in the white gloves John Willie, as he is affectionately known, has experienced the sad times and the glories, both in front of the cameras and behind the scenes. He has officiated all over the world, and been in charge of seven world snooker finals. He still considers his greatest thrill was to replace the balls for Cliff Thorburn in the world final of 1983 when the Canadian compiled the only TV maximum to be made in the Championship.

With a grown-up family of three sons and a daughter, John has left his native Wales, and settled in Shrewsbury. Life could have been different. At 17 he had a trial for Bolton Wanderers but the green pitch came second to the green baize. Snooker took over, and now he has no time for hobbies, but he thinks he could enjoy being a golfer! Always ready for a leg-pull, and a pint, he's a happy man on the circuit.

John Williams

HALL OF FAME

The younger of the two remarkable snooker-playing brothers (Joe being 12 years older), Fred Davis is today the doyen of the profession. He became a professional at the age of 17 in 1930 and after an illustrious career was awarded the OBE for his services to the game in 1977. Eight times World Snooker Champion, he is one of only two players (his brother being the other) to have won both World Billiards and World Snooker titles.

Having watched and worked with all the top stars since the 1940s, I can categorically say Fred was the most compact and solid player I have ever seen. With the disadvantage of poor eyesight from a young age, Fred originated the swivel lens specs; he also suffered until his thirties from having to live in the shadow of his flamboyant brother.

The brothers were entirely different characters. No parties for Fred, who was a non-smoker and non-drinker (today he enjoys a glass of wine). He couldn't be bothered with the inane questions all those in the limelight receive. The show over, his only thought was home. Fred's one outside interest has always been horse racing.

His wife Sheila was a terrific businesswoman and workaholic who, supported by Fred, owned and ran hotels in North Wales. Since she passed away, Fred Davis is content with the quiet life on his stud farm, where his daughters Lynne and Alison take care of the work and the horses.

———————————◆———————————

Fred Davis

The name Joe Davis will forever be synonymous with the game of snooker. He foresaw its potential when all others ridiculed it in favour of billiards. Against all odds he negotiated between players and governing body to organise the first World Snooker Championship back in 1927. Finding nine other entrants, he proved himself the best. With his winnings (£6 10s.) he bought a trophy – yes, the very same one presented today; the prize money, however, is very different! He held the title for twenty years until retiring from championship play in 1946.

The twentieth year of the Championship was to be Joe's crowning glory, culminating with the final at the Horticultural Hall, Westminster against Australia's Horace Lindrum. It was the first time the public had seen a match over 145 frames and they came in their thousands. After two weeks we knew the result – Davis 78, Lindrum 67. That final was my introduction to professional snooker. Joe and I became close friends and remained so until his death in 1978.

He married for the second time in 1945, to the vivacious musical comedy star, June Malo, and her influence brought him new strengths. Although from ordinary beginnings (he often dropped his aitches) he happily and regularly mixed with Lords and Dukes, he dressed immaculately (silk shirts and suits tailored in Savile Row) and was an astute businessman with a reputation for meanness. A good organiser and tough in argument, he had above all a terrific charisma – when Joe entered the room, everyone looked up!

In his earlier days Joe could be domineering to the point of arrogance and this sometimes caused friction with his fellow professionals, but he was always fair. He worked tirelessly, presenting, promoting and playing the game all over the world. To me he was an idol, a second father; and the undisputed King of Snooker.

Joe Davis

Horace Lindrum was born into a most extraordinary family. He was the fourth and last generation of the billiards-playing Lindrums, whose records and feats fill the record books, never to be beaten or equalled. Great-Grandfather and Grandfather, both Freds, were also champions at billiards. His uncle Walter was more than a champion, more a legend, and Horace was both Australian Professional Billiards and Snooker Champion, and a World Champion at snooker.

Although brought up on billiards (his records show over one thousand breaks of 1,000 or over), Horace pioneered snooker in a similar fashion to Joe Davis. He took his artistry to the most remote corners of the world from islands in the Far East, through India, South Africa, and of course Great Britain. Wherever he appeared it was the same story: 'When will you return and entertain us again?' people wanted to know. He was an attractive player – his boyish face and curly hair framed his twinkling eyes, and his ready smile and the chuckle in his voice all added up to a great personality.

He was double-jointed in all fingers which made him an expert at marbles. Able to apply amazing spin, he could play billiards without the aid of his cue; his trick shots were a joy to see.

The personality and charm of the youngest Lindrum naturally attracted the ladies. At the age of 37 he finally chose an English girl as his bride – an organising secretary at the Billiards Association, Miss Joy White (no relation to Jimmy). They married at St Martins-in-the-Fields, London in 1949, and I had the honour of being their best man. Joy was a great partner, tending his business affairs, organising his extensive tours and 'ghosting' his books. She also fulfilled motherhood – they had two lovely daughters. The great talent that Horace Lindrum possessed eventually took its toll. Ill health sadly came too early, and he died at the age of 62.

Horace Lindrum

Mention billiards anywhere, and almost immediately the name Walter Lindrum crops up. He was a phenomenon! The youngest of a family of four (two boys, two girls), he was the only Lindrum to be born in Western Australia – hence his names, Walter Albert. Like his father and elder brother, he was born left-handed.

Father (a champion himself) paid more attention to elder brother Fred in the boys' early days, coaching him to be a right-handed champion. He succeeded!

Walter, however, could not be kept away from the billiards table, and Dad soon recognised something special. As a perfectionist and serious-minded man he set the younger Lindrum to practise, playing one shot with only two balls for weeks on end.

Walter left school at 14 and immediately became a billiards professional (he had already compiled a 500 break in practice). At school he had been a keen sportsman and became a very proficient cricketer with many centuries to his credit. A decision had to be made and Dad encouraged the family obsession.

A boy champion at 15 (he made his first 1,000 break at 17), he toured Australia extensively taking all honours as he went. In 1929 he visited England for the first time and in his London début against Willie Smith set up a new world-record break of 3,262. Two years later against Joe Davis he made 4,137, a record that still stands today.

Walter Lindrum was a stockily built man completely dedicated to becoming the world's great billiardist. He had little concern for snooker. Had he taken it up in a big way, who can say he would not have gone as far as he did at billiards.

A modest and very friendly man, his one interest away from billiards was horse racing. Sometimes absent-minded and always disorganised, his genius gained him an OBE, and a 'command' to Buckingham Palace to meet King George V. When he died in 1960 he took billiards with him!

Walter Lindrum

No book of snooker characters would be complete without John Pulman. At 6ft 2in he stands pretty tall, and he's also head and shoulders above most in sociability. A great conversationalist and raconteur, John can keep any company amused for most of any evening (and night).

Eight times a winner of the World Professional snooker title, he actually held the crown for eleven years from 1957 to 1968. His reign was a difficult one. He saw little of the advantages a world champion deserves, for the game was at a low ebb and the championship was almost dormant for lack of promoters and sponsors.

Always a fighter – his Dad had taught him the hard way in his billiard club back in Exeter – the swashbuckling Pulman threw down the gauntlet to any challenger for his title, and successfully defended it seven times. Apart from reaching the top when the game was financially dead, John had the misfortune of a marriage break-up and a severe car accident that threatened his career. He never quite recaptured his old form.

He had an impeccable personal style, well-groomed hair and was always magnificently dressed, including diamond studs and cuff links (a grooming legacy from Joe Davis). His play was also elegant and his stance perfect, another throwback to his father's rigorous coaching. Like Fred Davis he needed specs and followed Fred's lead by using swivel lenses.

John finally retired from tournament play in the early 1980s. Today he is No. 1 commentator on the ITV team, and no-one has a better insight into the game. As he says himself, 'If you travel Pulman, you travel first-class.' He is doing just that.

John Pulman

Willie Smith was born in Darlington in 1886 and will always be regarded as the greatest all-round billiards player that ever lived. He played the type of game the ordinary player understood and attempted in local pubs and clubs. Almost by accident he drifted from his job as a linotype operator in Darlington to that of professional billiards player by accepting half-a-guinea expenses to play an exhibition in Middlesbrough. The dictatorial Billiards Association of the day stripped him of his amateur status and he never forgave them.

A colourful character with a ready cutting remark, Willie was at loggerheads with the establishment for most of his serious playing career, hence a lack of championship appearances. He won the world title at his first attempt in 1920, then missed the next two years, preferring to play more lucrative exhibitions. He took the title again in 1923 and promptly forgot championship play. Well aware he was No. 1 in the public eye he played a series of matches with the other four leading stars – Newman, Davis, McConachy and Lindrum – but their quick-scoring, close nursery cannon artistry increasingly annoyed him.

His feelings for snooker were much the same. When asked his thoughts on the game, he would say 'They should change the rules – *all* of them!' He mellowed with the years and in the early Fifties appeared annually at Leicester Square Hall, in a birthday match of mixed billiards and snooker against Joe Davis. His birthday luncheon was full of conversation about bygone days and amusing anecdotes. It was shared by no more than half a dozen, usually Bob and Alf Pearson, Joe Davis and yours truly. Willie consistently joked of a cash shortage but enjoyed the best cuisine. Holidays were taken at the same hotel in Cornwall for forty years.

Willie Smith outlived all his contemporaries, dying at his home in Leeds in 1980 at the wonderful age of 96. He left behind him the greatest all-round billiards break ever made – 2,743.

Willie Smith